# Branding Exposure Using
# Promotional Products

Get results quickly with the How-To-Guide of using promotional products.

Delia Biljon

Author
Delia Biljon
P.O. Box 51243
Musgrave
Durban
South Africa
4062

# Contents

# Foreword

I have run a very successful company called Delbi Promotions for years and have researched the fascinating industry of promotional products. There are so many companies starting up, but also many are closing down because they are simply not equipped to deal with the end buyer. They think that one simply takes an order and fulfils it – right? Wrong!

We need to know our customers' needs and more importantly, their objectives. Why hand out the promotional item in the first place if you are unable to measure the success of doing so.

Arm yourself with the knowledge to ensure that your promotional giveaways turn to "gold". Understand that ingenuity and knowledge can make or break a business. Learn how to create VALUE for your business. This book will help you with the basics of the industry and the uses for promotional products.

This book is a treasure trove of practical strategies that educate, motivate and inspire.

# The Promotional Product Industry

We will explore the basics of this industry, looking at what works and why.  You will not only learn good habits, you will also learn to ask the right questions.

The road to marketing your company is not particularly easy but if you travel it with determination, you will find yourself in a fascinating and rewarding business.

**The promotional products industry**
- Fun and exciting industry
- Good pay for good performance
- Unlimited growth potential
- Meeting interesting people
- Selling opportunities everywhere
- Flexible hours
- Interact with all types of businesses

As you get to know the promotional products industry, you will soon recognize that those who gravitate toward this creative industry are generally positive, enthusiastic people who enjoy working with ideas and people.

## What are promotional products?

Promotional products are merchandise items that often display an advertising or sales promotion message on them.  They are typically used in advertising and promotion communication vehicles, such as goodwill reminders, signs, gifts and incentives.  Promotional products include advertising specialities, premiums, recognition awards, business gifts and other identification applications.

## Advertising (Ad) specialities

Ad specialities have these key elements:
1. An advertising or promotional message;
2. Placed on, or with, a useful item; and
3. Given with no strings attached.

## Premiums

Give a useful item with some requirement to get another (for example, take a test drive for a free t-shirt) and the item becomes a premium. A premium is given as an incentive to do or buy something. Often premiums are imprinted and sometimes they are not. What makes an item a premium is the incentive.

## Recognition awards

Plaques, service pins, trophies, award jewellery and other gifts that signify performance are categorised as recognition awards. When these awards are used as incentives, such as in a safety campaign or sales competition, they are also premiums.

## Business gifts

These are the most common type of promotional item. They are most commonly given to customers or employees. Promotional gift giving could be to thank customers, to develop business, to recognise employee performance or long service.

## To sum up: promotional products are useful for:

- Tradeshows
- Customer goodwill and retention (as mentioned under "business gifts" above)
- Employee relations and events
- Brand awareness
- Public relations

- New customer / account generation
- Employee service awards
- Non profit programs
- Internal promotions
- New product / service introductions

You may use products such as jackets and caps, imprinted key rings as souvenirs, promotional inflatables, or balloons that serve as attention gainers at events.

## How do promotional products compare with advertising?

A simple way to think about advertising is to consider the difference between a shotgun blast and a rifle shot. Mass media advertising (newspaper, TV, radio, magazines and outdoor) is your shotgun variety. They aim at a general target and the message is widely scattered.

Promotional products on the other hand are tightly targeted, making use of direct mail, database marketing (mostly over the internet) by fax or phone. This form of marketing hits a precise, defined target audience.

# The promotional products industry

- The birth of the industry was the late 1800's
- Today, the promotional industry is worth $15.64 billion in sales.

## INDUSTRY SALES VOLUME IN BILLIONS

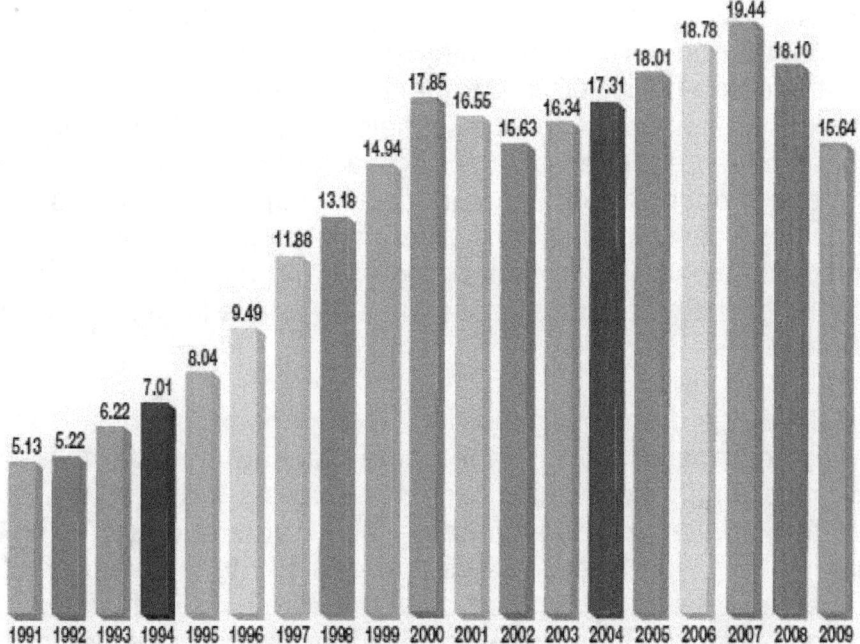

Data source: Information from the Promotional Products
Association International

Promotional products comprise useful items that are used in marketing and communication programs. The items include wearable's, writing instruments, calendars, drink ware and many other items, usually imprinted with a company's name, logo or message.

Distributor sales of promotional products in the US declined by 13.61% in 2008 to $15 638 571 468.  This is the lowest since 2002 and the sales volume is a direct reflection of the tough economy that affected advertising media across the board in 2009.  Although there is no data available in South Africa regarding the promotional product sales, key suppliers have noted a clear decrease in sales in 2009 due to the economy both internationally and locally.  The global financial crisis wiped out a number of economies so it is no surprise that the industry took a hit in 2009.  Larger companies in the US experienced smaller decreases in sales (2.35%) while smaller companies experienced a huge decrease of 22.62%.  A number of printing, packaging and health supply companies (dental, eye care, medical and veterinary supply) now report significant sales in promotional products and this could account for the smaller decrease in sales by the larger companies.

A 13.6% sales drop isn't good but in comparison to other media, it compares well.  Other media that saw considerable losses were print advertising, with newspapers losing 28.6% in advertising sales and consumer magazine and revenue dropping 18.1%.  Billboard sales dropped 15.6% last year and internet advertising, which had been growing by double digits in recent years, was down 3.4%.  The biggest surprise was a 15.6% drop in sales for direct mail, which hadn't previously had a loss in modern times.  Although the drop in sales for other media doesn't make matters better, it shows that the drop in promotional product sales was not abnormal.

# The players in the promotional industry

The promotional industry is divided into two distinct sections:
1. Suppliers
2. Distributors

The suppliers make up the production end of the industry. They are companies that manufacture, import, imprint or otherwise produce items offered for sale through distributors. Distributors are the sales representatives for the industry. Distributors are independent agents representing many competing suppliers.

# Top Promotional Product Categories

These products make up 73% of industry sales

- ❏ 31% Wearable's
- ❏ 10% Writing Instruments
- ❏ 7% Bags
- ❏ 6% Drink ware
- ❏ 6% Desk and Office Accessories
- ❏ 6% Calendars
- ❏ 4% Recognition Awards/Trophies/Jewellery
- ❏ 3% Computer related accessories

Some supply lines limit themselves to a select number of suppliers and others offer any item at the best price. You can meet the needs of the customer from any one of a number of competitive suppliers.

# Selling from a catalogue

Most promotional consultants sell from catalogues and a few samples. The consultants function is to find solutions that meet your objective. We will go into this a little later but the consultant should not fall into the habit of simply leaving the catalogue with you because you will get very confused with the choices. Rather tell your promotional consultant what your objective is and let them do the searching for you. Bear in mind that the promotional consultant will only offer you tried and tested promotions that have worked by many companies in the past. You may make the mistake of getting emotionally attached to an idea but it may not be the best idea to meet your objective. Never buy because you like a promotional item, instead buy because it will meet your objective of perhaps gaining a new client by creating the brand awareness.

In the catalogue, there is the product picture with its description. Always take note of the information in the catalogue and ask how long the orders take to fill, charges for special services, less-than minimum charges, costs for gift boxes, delivery charges etc. It is quite common for suppliers to change the product line year on year.

## Samples

Samples are wonderful selling tools. People like to hold and feel samples. Samples show the quality of the item better than pictures in a catalogue can. Ask the person that you are dealing with to supply a sample. Obviously they cannot afford to carry tons of samples so the trick is to pick your sample after checking its price first. If it fits all of the criteria, then as a final decision, see a sample first.

Remember that the item is less important than how it is used. Think of the promotional consultant as an idea pro rather than an item peddler.

# Marketing and Sales Tips

## Building relationships with your customers

- ❏ Take a cup of coffee to chat
- ❏ Buy them a book of value
- ❏ Send a postcard
- ❏ Remember birthdays
- ❏ Invite clients to lunch
- ❏ Share newspaper clippings
- ❏ Research company histories and send a cake on their birthday
- ❏ When you visit your clients, ask them:
  What they think of you as opposed to the competition;
  What they see themselves needing in the future;
  If they would buy or use your services again and if not, why not.  If yes, over what period of time;

  The answers to these questions will allow you to move forward from a position of knowledge.


## Publicity plan / Networking:

Publicity and networking helps you rise above your competition.  The more your name appears, the more your company name comes to mind when people think of promotions or events.  In addition, publicity can create unexpected opportunities and crown you as an expert.

## How to get going with cold calls?

Cold calling will be the basis of most of your initial work.  Very few people have warm feelings about cold calls. However, if you stick with your business ideas to the point of becoming a leader, there will come a day when you meet a person for the first time, discuss their business needs, suggest a idea and leave thousands richer.  Suddenly your cold calls will start feeling a lot warmer.

Remember that your goal is to learn as much as you can while cold calling and to make an appointment with the decision maker.  While you are cold calling and trying to set up these appointments, be prepared for some rejection but the reward at the end is so much richer!

**Things that you must do:**
1. See the people
2. Always learn what worked for them in the past
3. Use that knowledge to:
    a) sell to them
    b) sell to others
    c) adapt and improve the idea for other situations
4. Always use and give promotional products to those you meet
5. Concentrate less on closing the sale and more on opening relationships
6. Continually strengthen and deepen relationships through
    a) strong rapport
    b) creative ideas
    c) excellent service

When it comes to building goodwill and creating a sense of reciprocity, nothing works better than giving a small promotional gift.  It immediately shows friendliness and creates a small need for the recipient to do something nice for you in return.  Beyond stimulating people's need to reciprocate, giving promotional products gets your name into the marketplace where you want to do business.  It creates name recognition and strengthens a sense of familiarity.

Giving promotional products to clients, prospects and their employees is the most economical and effective way you can deliver your name and message to the people who are in a position to do business with you.

**Who do you call on in a company?**
Often you will speak to an owner, but in a large company there are many different divisions who order promotional products such as:

- The HR department
- Public relations or corporate communications departments
- Production / operations departments
- Sales / Marketing department
- Finance department

# What information do you need to give your promotional consultant?

You should be able to answer the following questions:
1. Who is the target audience?
2. What is the objective of the promotion?
3. What has been tried in the past and how did it work?
4. How many items and how much budget?
5. When, where and how will these promotional products be given out?
6. Who will be involved in the decision making? Whose approval do we need to move forward?

You will find a more in depth discussion on the information needed to create a marketing program.

# Distribution plans

What is a distribution plan?
Of all the advertising channels, promotional products alone do not have a built in distribution plan. TV, radio, newspapers, magazines, billboards, direct mail, and the internet all have message distribution included in the medium. So when you sell promotional products, it is wise to design a way for them to be given to the target audience.

Take for example a customer who orders 5000 caps. They are clearly intended to be given to a great many people. But how? If you like caps but do not have a plan for distributing them, you more than likely: 1) won't order more merchandise until you have used what you have and 2) will eventually conclude that promotional products don't work (because the undistributed products really don't).

You can avoid the risk of this happening by taking an interest the total program and ensuring effective distribution.

# What are promotional companies selling?

In the promotional products industry, there are 3 levels of selling:
1. Product selling
2. Idea selling
3. Program selling

## Product selling

This usually begins with a product that you like. You think that if you like it, your customers and prospects will like it. Then you go around showing it to them. Most promotional consultants find it easier to sell products. It is important to remember however that while it's a product that is being sold, it is the benefits that people are buying.  People do not buy promotional products because they are fascinating.  They buy them because using them will be beneficial to the business.

New sales people prefer selling a product because it is something tangible to show their prospect.  There is a big drawback to product selling and that is the susceptibility of competitive bidding.  In other words, you now have to compete on price.  There is a saying *"Products are sold on price. Ideas, rapport and service are sold at a profit"*.

**An example of product selling**
The consultant shows you a pen and hope that you like it.
One example of large pen orders:
Businesses use writing instruments.  They use them in the office and out on the field.  As they use them they lose them. Pens and pencils "walk out" with customers or get left in stores, they get "borrowed" by family or "lent" to friends who just need a pen "quickly".

If a business buys un-imprinted pens and pencils from a stationery shop, lost pens are a total loss.  If a business buys imprinted writing instruments, the lost pens amount to a gain because of their advertising value.  A pen left at a grocery store advertises the company's name to those who sign the cheque with the cashier.  Pens left at a customer's office serve as reinforcement of the business's name in that environment.

What is even more interesting is that because the pens and pencils are bought in quantity, rather than a few dozen at a time, the imprinted ones are nearly as inexpensive as the un-imprinted ones.  Sometimes they are even less expensive.

Smart businesses intentionally place writing instruments in places where they will be likely to receive high visibility.

Hotels know the value of providing imprinted pens for their guests and pens to seminar participants.

Smart department stores understand the value of making their printed pens available to women's clubs, attendees of special events and special groups.

Hospitals understand the value of leaving their pens in the offices of trusted physicians that use their hospital. This not only improves the relationship between the hospital and the physician but also raises the profile of the hospital in the patient's eyes because of its association with trusted physicians.

The point of these examples is that since businesses use writing instruments anyway, they might as well use imprinted writing instruments and reap the additional benefit of increased awareness.

## Idea selling

Idea selling is more complicated than product selling because it requires a general understanding of the product and of how the client's business works. One will need to understand the client's goals and what obstacles they face. For instance, speciality advertising such as building name recognition or encouraging referrals. This form of selling requires insight into specific promotional or communication problems each customer might be facing and then solving those problems using promotional products.

## Program selling
**How does program selling relate to idea selling?**

Program selling has its roots in idea selling and like idea selling can be simple or complicated. Just as idea selling requires the insights needed to do well in product selling, program selling incorporates the skills and techniques of both product selling and idea selling. In fact, program selling is actually idea selling with a systematic approach. While idea selling might be selling creative patches for business dilemmas, program selling is creating a quilt of solutions, fitting a number of patches together.

A program is a systematically executed promotional products campaign that motivates a target audience to achieve a desired goal.

**Types of programs**
Dealer / distributor
Safety incentive
Employee service awards and recognition
Sales motivation
Company store
Casual day / uniform
Direct mail

**Program opportunities**
Admin
- Suggestions
- VIP business gifts
- Special events, sponsored charities
Manufacturing
- Safety
- Production goals
- Quality incentives
HR
- Employee recognition
- Employee recruiting, retention

- Service awards
- Company store
- Casual day / uniforms

Marketing and sales department
- Distribution chain incentives
- Sales incentives
- Customer loyalty

Program selling requires strategic thinking but is the ultimate goal for any promotional consultant because they will add tremendous VALUE for their client.

Basic steps to follow in program selling:

1. Define specific objectives. This is the first and most important step in defining and designing an incentive based program. Simply answer this question: "What do we want to accomplish with this program?"

2. Identify the audience to be reached.

3. Agree on a budget.

4. Determine a workable implementation plan.

5. Create a theme for the promotion.

6. Develop promotional messages to support the theme.

7. Select the appropriate promotional products.

8. Establish a way of measuring results.

So there it is – some insights into the promotional product world. You have a starting point so make the most of it. Of course, real learning comes from action so get out there and give it your best shot.

Other useful discussion points that the staff and clients discuss at my company (Delbi Promotions):

# Questions are the answer

The Diagnostic Approach:
- Examine the patient
- Diagnose the problem
- Prescribe the solution

Rapport Building Questions

1. What is the biggest sales and marketing issue you are dealing with right now?
2. Where do you need to see some quick improvement?
3. What sort of business gifts do you use?
4. What is the primary thing that you would like me to help you with?
5. What sort of events do you have coming up in the next 30, 60 and 90 days?
6. What are the biggest challenges you face in promoting your business right now?
7. What is the most effective promotion you have done?
8. What is the least effective promotion you have done?

Rapport Building Tools

1. Useful and targeted promotional products – get this on

your customer's desk and tie the product into a message.
2. Email or printed newsletter – help people understand how to use promotional products to position their brand.
3. Position your staff and yourself as an expert.
4. Audio and video pod cast – Read an email with a microphone or use a webcam and post ideas to your website. Also send an email with that link.
5. Book on effective use of promotional products – give this to your clients or use quotes from the book.
6. Excerpts on books.
7. Gift related to client's interests or industry.
8. An interesting article you have written or read.
9. Random sample of an appropriate new product. Perhaps with your clients logo on it or even a virtual sample.
10. Details on a successful person you have read about.
11. A recommendation on a program that clients need and want.

## Marketing our media vs. other media

- Ours is a 19 billion dollar industry
- Our media is bigger than cable TV and outdoor advertising
- Promotional products can engage all five senses:
  Touch – weight or texture
  Sight – we can see the product
  Sound – the sound of the item (pen click for example)
  Smell – scented products
  Taste - branded chocolate

Promotional companies are not an interruption! People love receiving promotional gifts. Try a marketing SMS – that is an interruption!

# PROMOTIONAL PRODUCTS:
## IMPACT ON COMPANY

*A survey of business travellers at DFW Airport*

In a nutshell:

Promotional products furnish advertisers with advantages that may not be available in other media:

- High recall – the name of the advertiser is remembered

- Repeated exposure to the ad message

- A more favourable impression of the advertiser

Promotional products can drive a message far beyond traditional media. Some participants give the item away but this provides excellent pass along exposure to the advertiser similar to that of magazine advertising. The frequency of the promotional products use is tantamount to advertising exposure. In media measurement, the greater the frequency of exposure, the lower the cost per impression.

Reach:

- 71% are business people reported having received a promotional product in the last 12 months

Recall:

- 76.1% of the respondents could recall the advertiser's name on the product that they received in the past 12 months

- In comparison, participants were asked if they had read a newspaper or magazine in the past week. 80% of the participants said yes, but only 53.5% of them could recall the name of a single advertiser

Repeated exposure:

55% of the participants kept their promotional products for more than a year. This means repeated exposure over a long period of time.

---

*Contact Delia Biljon on 031 566 4148 or email delia@delbipromotions for a detailed report or for more information on Promotional Product Impact and Branding.*

# PROMOTIONAL PRODUCTS:
# IMPACT AS AN ADVERTISING

*A study conducted by university researches*

In a nutshell:

Promotional products:

- May be effectively employed as a stand-alone advertising medium (second to television)

- Add to the media mix, creating impact by supplementing other advertising media such as television and print

- Are a useful information and reminder medium

- Enhance impressions about both the brand and product

- Contribute to consumer intent to buy

## Reach:

The research was conducted on the most critical demographic group ages 18-34 years. Those in this age group are the most difficult for marketers to reach and if the promotional products have an impact on this critical group then the utility of the medium is likely to be expandable to other age segments.

## Method:

Participants in the study were exposed to three forms of advertising – television, print and promotional products. They were then asked to complete a questionnaire measuring their perceptions of the advertising.

In this study, groups who were exposed to promotional products tended to rate the message more positively than those groups not exposed to a promotional product. In some instances, the use of a promotional product as the ad medium alone achieved maximum impact, up to 69% in increased brand interest and 84% in creating a good impression of the brand.

Interestingly, promotional products were the second most preferred source of information following television advertising.

*Contact Delia Biljon on 031 5664148 or email delia@delbipromotions for a detailed report or for more information on Promotional Product Impact and Branding.*

# What Clients Want

**Company Reputation**
Not what we say – it is what we do
**Sales Rep's Product Knowledge**
Can't know everything about each of 700 000 products but must know where to go to find the product

**Time Saving Benefit**
Customer's time is valuable
We must save them time
Convey benefits to them
Think of ideas to grow their business

**Ease of Contacting the Sales Rep**
Be available and if voicemail, phone right back

**Never wait until back in the office.**
Use technology to improve communication

**Ability to Supply Custom Work**
You must be a detailed person
Your ability to 'handle it' will be your biggest advantage
Take an idea from concept – finish/delivery and you will be better than competitors

**Variety of Product Selection and Options**
Provide 'intelligent' and thoughtful ideas
Too many options are not good
Provide samples

Have good suppliers with great products

## Easy Access to Product and Price Info
It must be easy for the customer to get information from you
You must vouch for the product
Provide clients with better results than they can get on their own – if not walk away

## All Charges Clearly Explained
Be clear upfront
Tell them the process
Tell about screen posies, overrun charges or shipping

## Competitive Pricing
Cheaper is not the top issue to the client
It is not about the lowest pricing, it is about competitive pricing
Always assume what is in their best interest and yours – good quality products at a reasonable price, delivered on time by someone they like

## Timely Response to Customer Concerns
Know what is happening every step of the way and let the client know. If there is a problem:
Match client's intensity (they are concerned, you are concerned)
Say sorry – what is the problem
Position problem as unusual
Take ownership of problem
Follow up immediately – if you say you will call back in 30 minutes, call back in 20 minutes

## Prompt and Timely Delivery of Orders
Get the right suppliers who won't let you down
If you can't, your business is doomed

# How Things Work – Understanding Artwork and Printing

It is important for your client's image that their corporate brand or identity is always consistent.

Many suppliers offer in-house art and design services for a fee. In many cases, creating art is as simple as utilising services that are already in place.

## Art vs. Artwork

While art may be considered anything that is creative and artistic, artwork adheres to accepted guidelines and professional procedures (sometimes called standards) so that suppliers can reproduce it, either on paper or on a variety of promotional products.

When re-creating an existing company logo, the goal is to duplicate the original as precisely as possible.

It is extremely important to obtain client approval on a paper copy (proof) that depicts the logo as it is to be imprinted, spelling out each colour exactly before the job is printed.

## Who Owns the Art?

Chances are your client owns all rights in and to his or her logo. This means that you can only reproduce that logo on a promotional item with the full consent and permission of your client.

To avoid possible copyright issues when contracting an artist to create an advertising logo or message for you or your client, it is a good idea to use a "work for hire" agreement.

## Electronic Arts Formats Explained

It's a good idea to "achieve" your client's art and logo by saving it in several electronic formats. Make sure that each contains the company name and contact information.

• **VECTOR GRAPHIC FILE** is a method of image generation using a number of straight lines and/or arcs of different length and angular orientation. This format is highly recommended, as it offers the most flexibility and is used by most promotional product suppliers. Commonly used programs include CorelDraw and Adobe Illustrator. Vector files should be saved in their native format with embedded fonts and also as both an esp. file and PDF file with fonts converted to curves or paths.

• **A BITMAP** is a digital representation of an image where a grid is used to indicate whether each point of the image black, white or a colour. If a logo or message has been created as a bitmap (or your existing logo as been scanned), save the file in its native format, for example: .bmp, .tif or .pct. For this file to be considered acceptable, it must be at least 100% of the printed size for black and white images and 200% of size for colour. Popular bitmap manipulation programs include Adobe Photoshop, and Corel Photo paint.

These programs will also usually require a recreation of logos at an additional cost.

**Can't you just get the logo from our website?**
Probably not...at least not without additional charges. Graphics on websites are designed to load as fast as possible, and usually lack sufficient quality for reproduction on promotional products. While web graphics may be adapted to work, it may very well involve recreating the logo, which will almost certainly result in additional costs.

**Industry Charges and Buzzwords**
Like most industries, the promotional products industry has its own unique terms and buzzwords. Even the most seasoned professionals may sometimes fail to fully explain what they mean.

This section is designed to provide you with basic information that will help you to better communicate with your clients and suppliers to achieve the results you desire. It covers just a few of the most common terms and decorating processes. Keep in mind; this is an area that changes rapidly with technological advances. Your best suppliers can guide you through the maze of decorating techniques to ensure that your client's logo or message is presented in the most favorable manner.

**Common Setup Procedures and Charges**

• **CAMERA READY ARTWORK** – the traditional reference to artwork that is complete and ready to use without further modification. "Camera Ready" often consists of a black image on white paper, exactly 100% of the printed size, on high quality photographic paper. While many office laser printers are capable of creating acceptable results, most ink jet printers are not. Remember, the final result will depend entirely on the quality of the artwork.

• **COLOUR SEPERATIONS** – With multi-colour artwork, there is a separate piece of camera ready art for each printed colour, and registration marks on each sheet to ensure that all the colours line up to create the desired result.

• **FILM** – Camera ready art is often scanned or actually photographed to create either a film positive or a film negative that may be used in the creation of a screen or die. It more closely resembles the film of an X-ray than the film of a small camera.

• **SPOT COLOUR** – Each specific colour of ink is printed right where it's needed. What you see is what you get. For example, if you are printing a three colour logo of green, blue and yellow, only green, blue and yellow ink would be used.

• **PROCESS COLOUR** – This process mixes the four basic colours of cyan, magenta, yellow and black (CMYK) to create nearly any colour allowing for the appearance of a "full colour" imprint, using just four basic colours of ink.

• **ELECTRONIC ARTWORK** – a computer generated file of Artwork. Everything necessary to generate colour separated, camera ready art.

- **SETUP COST** – The charge to make a job ready for production.
- **COLOUR MATCH CHARGE** – The cost to mix inks to match a specific colour. The industry standard for colour matching is the "Pantone" or "PMS" colour matching system.

**Methods of Decoration**

Here is a brief overview of the most common processes used to decorate promotional products, along with their pros and cons:

- **SCREEN PRINTING**: Setup involves using a combination of light and chemicals to "burn" the image into a pattern on the screen. The screens are then set up and registered, and ink is then physically pushed through the pattern in the screen to imprint the design on a promotional product. The ink may then be "cured" by running the printed item under a heating element.
  o **PROS**: Screen printing is relatively quick, affordable and long lasting. It can reproduce fine detail, colour matching, and can be used on many surfaces, including glassware and textiles.
  o **CONS**: With spot colour printing, each colour requires an additional screen and/or set up, often resulting in additional charges. Process colour printing is possible, but colour separations can be very costly, and getting a correct, consistent finished result can be tricky. Flash curing individual inks may also be necessary when printing colour on colour (particularly white on dark items.) This may result in additional "flash" charges.
- **PAD PRINTING**: Setup involves rendering the image onto a rubber pad template, similar to a soft rubber "stamp". Ink is then transferred from the rubber pad onto the promotional product.
  o **PROS**: Pad printing can be used to print on irregular

surfaces, like golf balls or even walnuts. Colour matching is also possible.

o **CONS**: Multiple colour printing is not always possible, and pad printing is best suited to smaller imprint areas.

• **EMBROIDERY**: Setup involves telling an embroidery machine exactly where to place each stitch. Thread is sewn into a pattern, creating the logo or message.

o **PROS**: Embroidery is perceived as an "upscale" option, providing a rich and sophisticated look.

o **CONS**: It is not always possible to reproduce fine detail or shading in an embroided logo. In some cases, modification of the logo may be necessary.

"Digitization", "punching" or "tape" charges (embroidery setup) can be more expensive than other types of setup charges. These costs are usually based on the number of stitches (i.e. larger designs mean more stitches and a higher price.)

• **OFFSET PRINTING:** Setup involves the creation of a plate or template. An inked image is set off from a printing plate onto a rubber blanket which in-turn is transferred to paper.

o **PROS:** The process provides exact reproduction, and is inexpensive in larger runs.

o **CONS:** Offset printing is limited to flat paper products.

• **TRANSFER PRINTING:** In this process, transfers are created, utilizing special printers and sublimation inks. Heat and pressure transfer the image onto the promotional product.

o **PROS:** Full colour is possible, and digital printing allows this to be done, even in smaller quantities.

o **CONS:** Cannot be used on all surfaces. Limited to use on promotional products designed to receive sublimation inks (i.e. certain t-shirts, glassware, mugs, mouse pads and plaques.)

• **ETCHING AND ENGRAVING:** Setup may involve creating a template or programming the laser (or other equipment) on where to cut. In this process, a hand tool, chemical, laser or abrasive is used to remove material and etch or cut the logo or message into the product. This process can be used on a variety of materials including metal, glass, stone and wood.

o **PROS:** Beautiful, three-dimensional look.

o **CONS:** Setup can be costly, and no colours are involved, unless another decoration process is also used.

• **HOT STAMPING, EMBOSSING AND DEBOSSING:** Setup begins with production of a metal die, and costs vary according to size. The die is used to press the logo or message into the promotional item.

o **PROS:** These processes provide excellent results on vinyl, leather and even some paper products.

o **CONS:** It is not always possible to reproduce fine detail or shading using these processes.

# APPENDIX

## *Opening Ideas*

# Car Dealers

### Target Audience:
Any potential new car buyer, who may be observing other vehicles in traffic.

### Objective:
To create an association between cars and where to buy them.

### Item:
License disc holders
Car decals

### Distribution:
On new and used cars before they are purchased.

### Target Audience:
Purchaser of a new or used car.

### Objective:
To ensure continued patronage, stimulate third-party recommendations; create goodwill to smooth over future problems in advance and overcome "buyer remorse".

### Item:
First aid kits
Road atlases / maps
Road flares
Key tags

### Distribution:

Give out as a "thank you for doing business with us", and/or a "thank you for recommending us to your friends in the future".

## Financial Institutions

### Target Audience:

Current bank customers

### Objective:

Identify, third-party endorsements and insurance

### Item:

Desk and wall calendars (consider a custom picture of the bank on the calendar)

### Distribution:

Given to retail and commercial accounts as gifts that serve as year-long "signs."

### Target Audience:

Current customers and community at large

### Objective:

Identification and insurance

### Item:

Imprinted pens for common use in the bank

### Distribution:

By using imprinted pens rather than pens from a stationery store, the bank can realise goodwill and extra advertising when pens are kept by customers

# Health clubs and Spas

## Target Audience:
Prospects

## Objective:
Incentive and identity

## Item:
Wearables – t-shirts, headbands, wristbands, caps

## Distribution:
Offer as part of a trial membership advertised in newspaper and given as incentives to join the club

## Target Audience:
Current customers

## Objective:
Souvenirs

## Item:
Workout bags
Visors
Towels
T-shirts
Jackets
Pens
Desk items with a clever exercise quote

**Distribution:**

Sold in a shop inside the club

## Hospitals

**Target Audience:**

Community-at-large

**Objective:**

Identification and invitation to promote emergency room facilities (more than one-third of hospital admissions come through their emergency rooms)

**Item:**

Calendars
Fridge magnet emergency numbers

**Distribution:**

Delivered to public businesses such as gas stations, schools, and recreational facilities in the area

**Target Audience:**

Residents and staff at nursing homes / senior citizens centres

**Objective:**

Identification, invitation and goodwill

**Item:**

Calendars
Note pads
Wall clocks
Emergency number fridge magnets or stickers

**Distribution:**

Distributed to visitors, residents and staff as part of a health care seminar at nursing homes and senior citizens

# Hotels

**Target Audience:**

Meeting and convention planners

**Objective:**

Identity, invitation and goodwill

**Item:**

Portfolios
Executive desk items (laser engraved pen sets)
Cube pads
Custom calendars
Wearables

**Distribution:**

Direct mail advertising or given with personal sales calls or when client visits hotel to see facilities

# Travel agencies

**Target Audience:**

Business travel reservation decision makers (often also secretaries)

## Objective:
Identity, invitation and insurance

## Item:
Desk calendars
Pen and pencil holders
Coasters
Mugs
Personalised sticky notes
Paper clip holders

## Distribution:
Given in person with sales presentation and through the mail as a thank you follow-up

## Target Audience:
Travel groups on an organised tour

## Objective:
Identity, invitation and insurance

## Item:
T-shirts
Scarves
Name badges
Luggage tags
Travel cases
Pens
Hats
Luggage stickers

## Distribution:
Given as part of travel packet for a trip

# THE END

www.ingramcontent.com/pod-product-compliance
Lightning Source LLC
Chambersburg PA
CBHW051301170526
45165CB00004B/1807